I AM
AFFIRMATIONS

By Larry Bell

Illustrations by Annie Wilkinson

Published by Larry Bell LLC

For information about special discounts for bulk purchases, please contact Larry Bell LLC sales: business@larrybellllc.com

ISBN: 979-8-218-20158-6

Printed in the United States of America

To Little Larry

You are a creator; you create with
every thought.

I am valuable.

I am abundant.

I am clear-minded.

I am eager.

I am decisive.

I am appreciated.

I am energized.

I am determined.

I am talented.

I am confident.

I am strong.

I am healthy.

I am nourished.

I am able.

I am happy.

I am empowered.

I am Worthy.

I am loved.

Meet Larry

Larry Bell, a first-time children's book author from Georgia, has always had a passion for uplifting others.

After years of working in the finance industry, Larry decided to pursue his dream of becoming a children's book author. He drew inspiration from his own childhood experiences and the joys and challenges of developing self-worth.

Larry's debut children's book, "I Am Affirmations", serves to remind young readers that anything you can imagine is yours to be, do, or have.

16192987R00019